A PARRAGON BOOK
Published by Parragon Book Service Ltd, Unit 13-17 Avonbridge Trading Estate,
Atlantic Road, Avonmouth, Bristol BS11 9QD
Produced by The Templar Company plc, Pippbrook Mill,
London Road, Dorking, Surrey RH4 1JE
Copyright © 1995 Parragon Book Service Limited
All rights reserved
Printed and bound in Italy
ISBN 0-75250-872-5

PICTURE TALES

Cinderella

Illustrated by Brian Bartle

‖ •PARRAGON• ‖

Once there was a poor

called Cinderella, who lived

with her father, stepmother

and her two ugly stepsisters.

They made her work hard to

keep the clean.

One day an arrived

from the . The Prince was

holding a grand ball.

The were very

excited, but knew she

would not be allowed to go.

On the day of the ball, the
 put on their finest
 and left sitting sadly

by the .

But in a flash, Cinderella's

fairy godmother appeared!

"You shall go to the ball," she said to  . "Fetch me a  , four white  , a fat  and four  ."  did as she was told at once, and soon returned.

With a wave of her , the

fairy godmother changed the

 into a , the

into , the into a

coachman, and the

into footmen. With another

wave of her 🪄 she changed

Cinderella's old rags into a

beautiful 👗 , with glass 👠

for her 🦶 . "Leave before

midnight," she warned, "or it

will all change back!"

 had a wonderful time at the ball, and danced with the all night. He thought she was the most beautiful girl in the world. But then the struck midnight.

fled from the .

But when she got outside, her had turned back into a , and there were four , four  and a  beside it!

ran away into the night,

but she dropped a glass

on the  steps.

The found the glass

 lying on the  , and

declared he would search

every in the land until he

found the beautiful it

belonged to, and then he

would marry her. So the

searched far and wide, but

though many tried to

get the little on their

 , it did not fit any of them.

At last he arrived at

Cinderella's  . The

tried hard to make the fit,

but it was impossible.

Finally it was  turn , and the slipped on easily. The had found her at last!

They were married next day and lived happily ever after!